I0448806

Federal Accounting Standards Advisory Board

Financial Reporting Model Task Force

Report to the FASAB

Electronic, Web-Based Financial Reporting

December 22, 2010

Table of Contents

December 22, 2010

Federal Accounting Standards Advisory Board
441 G Street NW
Washington DC 20548

The United States government released its annual financial report yesterday. Although the report presents information that is important to citizens as they form judgments about the fiscal future of the federal government under current policy, it is unlikely that many Americans will be aware of its existence and availability. Because the nation is currently engaged in crucial debates about the appropriate response to its near-term and long-term fiscal imbalance, the annual financial report is now more relevant to citizens, political leaders, and analysts than ever before.

Further, the recent celebration of the 20th anniversary of the Chief Financial Officer's (CFO) Act offers a clear reminder of the considerable improvement in federal financial reporting over the past two decades. However, the challenge of effectively delivering the information to users remains unfinished. The recommendations we transmit today are intended to considerably strengthen the presentation, availability, and usefulness of critical financial information about the federal government to citizens. Our recommendations build on the existing financial reporting model and would lead to easier access to more understandable federal financial information.

To best meet the public's needs and improve government transparency and accountability, we recommend that the federal government adopt an electronic, Web-based method of communicating information about the financial condition and performance of the federal government. This change in the medium of delivery would permit user needs to be met more quickly and at lower cost than the paper-based, static method currently in use today.

In addition, we recommend reporting:

- program performance measures and accomplishments of the federal government;
- net cost and spending by function and department; and
- intergovernmental financial dependency measures.

Also, to improve their usefulness, we are recommending several other specific changes to the presentation of information in the present financial reports.

We recommend further that the FASAB's sponsors take action in the near term to establish a Web site and publicize its availability. Absent a sustained effort to inform the public about the new site, even the best Web site is unlikely to be used to a great extent.

In developing a consensus on the content and recommendations in this report, Task Force members offered a range of perspectives. While there were major compromises by at least one member in arriving at our final recommendations, each member agrees strongly on the urgent need to improve the ability of the U.S. government to communicate effectively with all of its stakeholders. This urgency is perhaps best illustrated by the current national discussion on the need to assure the long-term fiscal sustainability of the federal government and the related specific need for stakeholders to assess the impact of alternative courses of action. The Task Force members believe that this report offers an effective and reasonable approach to improving public understanding of the financial condition and performance of the national government.

Jonathan D. Breul, Executive Director, IBM Center for the Business of Government

Patricia E. Healy, Executive Consultant, CGI

Michael J. Hettinger, Executive Director of Practice Planning and Marketing, Global Public Sector, Grant Thornton LLP

John H. Hummel, Partner and Federal Segment Leader, KPMG LLP

Edward J. Mazur, Senior Advisor for Public Sector Services, Clifton Gunderson, L.L.P

Marvin Phaup, Director, Federal Budget Reform Initiative, The Pew Charitable Trusts

Al Runnels, Deputy Chief Financial Officer, Department of the Treasury

Jeffrey C. Steinhoff, Executive Director, KPMG Government Institute, and Managing Director, KPMG LLP

Sheila A. Weinberg, founder and CEO, the Institute for Truth in Accounting

The objective of the Financial Reporting Model Task Force was to increase users' access to and understanding and use of financial information in the Consolidated Financial Report (CFR) of the federal government, while avoiding costly requirements that do not add value. To help achieve this objective, the task force developed 10 recommendations for the FASAB and its sponsors. While the task force primarily focused on government-wide reporting, recommendations 4, 5, and 8 also apply to agencies.

Recommendation 1: Adopt an Electronic, Web-Based Reporting Method

Move away from paper-based reporting and adopt an electronic, Web-based reporting method. Technology has fundamentally changed the way information is communicated. Print media are losing ground to the electronic World Wide Web. The public relies increasingly on digital devices, complex networks, and interactive media to obtain information on-demand. The task force expects this pattern in how people obtain information will continue to accelerate. Accordingly, financial reporting needs to switch from a paper-based, static reporting model to an electronic, dynamic form that is readily available online. It should also link the financial performance of the federal government in the CFR to that of its component agencies by providing all federal financial statements and program performance measures through a central Web site that enables users to quickly find the information of greatest interest.

Recommendation 2: Explore How Best to Report Additional Government-wide Performance Information

Explore how best to report additional government-wide program performance in management's discussion and analysis (MD&A) of the CFR or in another electronic government-wide presentation. The nation is engaged in deliberations to determine the federal government's future role in the economy and society. Program performance measures presented within the CFR could potentially help inform the national debate, especially if structured to provide information on such matters as: the government's effectiveness in achieving planned goals, and the economy and efficiency of government operations.

Recommendation 3: Present a Functional Statement of Net Cost in the CFR with Departmental Net Cost by Function as RSI

Present net cost and spending (outlays) by function as a basic financial statement and present net cost by function and department (or agency) in RSI. The current statement of net cost in the CFR presents net costs by agency. However, users focus on the cost of programs rather than the agency that conducts them. In addition, many users prefer spending data and are unaware that sometimes large differences exist between what is spent on a program and what a program costs. Presenting net cost by function and department (or agency) in RSI would allow users to identify the departments most relevant to the functions of interest to them.

Recommendation 4: Establish Minimum Requirements for a Statement of Spending

Establish minimum requirements for fair presentation of a Statement of Spending by agencies. We understand that the CFO Council is developing a Statement of Spending for agencies. At a minimum, a statement of spending for agencies and government-wide should: (a) be designed to help the public learn *where* and *how* their tax dollars are being spent, (b) present spending data in relation to net cost (covered in recommendation #3), and (c) include an explanation of the differences between spending and net cost.

Recommendation 5: Include Intergovernmental Financial Dependency Reporting in RSI

Include summary-level information on intergovernmental financial dependency (i.e., direct flows, indirect flows, and obligations held as investments), organized by state, in RSI. Intergovernmental financial dependency is the reliance of one level of government on another level for direct financial flows, or indirect financial flows derived from the purchases of goods and services and/or payments to individuals within a governmental jurisdiction by another level of government. Such dependency can also be associated with the holding of the financial obligation of one level of government by another as an income-producing asset.

The nation's critical programs, such as addressing health care needs and countering terrorism, involve the joint efforts of all levels of government. The federal government relies on state and local government management and resources to deliver these national programs. Accordingly, the fiscal health and policy decisions of each level of government have become significantly interdependent. To the extent state and local governments face fiscal challenges that impair their ability to carry out federal programs, there is a fiscal risk to the federal government as demonstrated by the hundreds of billions of dollars of recovery funding provided to state and local government. And conversely, to the extent the federal government curtails its spending in response to its own fiscal gap state and local governments' financial condition would be significantly affected.

Recommendation 6: Enhance the Information Value of the Reconciliation of Net Operating Cost and Unified Budget Deficit Statement through Re-labeling

Change the labels on the Reconciliation of Net Operating Cost and Unified Budget Deficit Statement so that the statement better helps readers understand the differences between the most commonly reported measure of government results – the deficit – and the accrual basis results. For example, headings such as "add excess of expenses over budget outlays," should be added to help readers understand which amounts are included or not included in the Unified Budget Deficit.

Recommendation 7: Reclassify the Information in the Statement of Changes in Cash Balance from Unified Budget and Other Activities

Reclassify the information on changes in the cash balance from the unified budget and other activities. The Statement of Changes in Cash Balance from Unified Budget and Other Activities is currently a basic financial statement. The information it provides should be presented instead as a schedule in the notes or in RSI because its main value is to provide an operational context for the financial statements. This would reduce the number of basic financial statements without reducing availability of currently reported information.

Recommendation 8: Re-orient the Balance Sheet Display and Enhance the Related MD&A Discussion

Change the format of the balance sheet such that the "bottom line" is "net position." This would focus users' attention on how the comparative values of assets and liabilities produce the resulting net position. Related discussions in MD&A should highlight why and how the assets of the government are important to the ongoing operations of the government and also identify and categorize the stakeholders that are reliant on the government meeting its liabilities and obligations.

Recommendation 9: Explain the Difference between Net Position and Fiscal Gap

Add explanatory text to the balance sheet to help readers understand the difference between net position and fiscal gap. Net position shown in the balance sheet provides a current view of the federal government's financial health by focusing on present resources (assets) and obligations (liabilities). Fiscal gap [1] is a broader "forward-looking view" that focuses on the imbalance between present as well as future resources and obligations.

Recommendation 10: Establish a Federal Financial Information Web Site and Raise Awareness of Federal Financial Information

Establish a central Web site for federal financial information and inform the public of its availability. Ultimately, the success of the previous recommendations requires raising public awareness of federal financial reports and the information they provide. Currently, the public is not aware that financial reports exist and some groups are building their own federal financial information Web sites to inform public debates.[2] Diverse Web sites and information sources that report "federal" financial information can be confusing to the public. A Web site would enable the federal government to take advantage of existing technologies and help identify improvements that may be needed. In addition, the government should undertake an initiative to increase awareness of the new federal Web site.

---

[1] Fiscal gap reported in the Sustainability Statement is the net present value of projected spending minus projected receipts, adjusted for the decrease or increase in public debt required to maintain public debt at or below the target percentage of gross domestic product for the stated projection period.

[2] For example, see http://www.annualreportusa.com/.

Context

Prior to the CFO Act of 1990, federal financial management systems were fragmented and incompatible and there was a negative public perception of federal financial information.[3] Since that time, agencies have improved systems and controls such that most are now able to prepare financial statements in conformity with generally accepted accounting principles (GAAP). Agencies now present financial reports[4] as printed documents and as printable documents on their individual Web sites. Although the achievements to date have helped to provide the public with comprehensive information about the financial health of the federal government, the current reporting model could be enhanced by focusing on the new ways individuals obtain information. The public's desire to obtain information rapidly requires the use of new technologies to deliver financial information.

FASAB research indicated that 42 percent of citizens would like to use the Internet to receive financial information about the federal government.[5] Internet users tend to scan text for information they expect to find instantaneously. Also, because of dramatic advancements in technology, the general public can have information readily available through integrated data capturing, where data becomes machine-readable rather than being read by an individual and reentered into another device. For example, Recovery.gov presents Recovery Act spending information in a citizen-friendly format. Citizens can use highly interactive maps, charts, and graphs to review information on Recovery Act projects in their state and zip code. Also, the Web site's Download Center provides access to the data behind the interactive maps, charts, and graphs and permits users to create their own reports.

Establishment of the Financial Reporting Model Task Force

In April 2010, the FASAB established the Financial Reporting Model Task Force (hereafter referred to as the "task force"). The objective of the task force was to examine the current federal financial reporting model and make actionable recommendations to increase users' understanding, access, and use of federal financial information while avoiding costly requirements that do not add value. The task force began by focusing on government-wide financial reporting and

---

[3]Comptroller General of the United States Charles A. Bowsher, Financial Management Reform, Before the Committee on Government Operations, U.S. House of Representatives, (Washington, D.C. September 17, 1990).
[4] Financial reports are commonly referred to as Performance and Accountability Reports or Agency Financial Reports.
[5] FASAB, *User Needs Study: Citizens*, April 12, 2010, found at http://www.fasab.gov/conceptsfinan.html.

considered: data from the FASAB user needs study and its relationship to the financial reporting objectives (see Appendix I: Financial Reporting Objectives), the information presented in the Fiscal Year 2009 CFR, and financial reporting issues raised by FASAB members.

The task force's efforts began with the government-wide report because, for external users, such as citizens and public interest groups that may serve as citizen-intermediaries, it is a likely starting point in the search for federal financial information. During the FASAB user needs study, staff conducted focus group discussions which showed that citizens are not likely to be aware of individual federal departments and agencies. Therefore, they are most likely to be introduced to federal financial reports through a single financial report for the U.S. federal government.

In reaching conclusions on the importance of outreach to users, the task force considered the following matters:

- Citizens were not aware that the federal government and agencies prepared audited financial statements, and some federal executives and managers had not seen their own agency's financial statements.

- Citizens would like to use the Internet to obtain financial information about the federal government.

- Both cash and accrual basis accounting appear to be needed to provide the information users need.

- Citizens and some federal executives and managers noted difficulty in understanding information in financial reports. They believed that the documents are intended for accountants or economists rather than citizens and managers. In some instances, executives and managers develop their own data and reports.

- Congress seeks timely, easy to understand information to address issues.

In addition, the task force organized a subgroup and reviewed the contents of the Fiscal Year 2009 CFR which included A Message from the Secretary of the Treasury, MD&A, Statement of the Acting Comptroller General of the United States, Financial Statements, Disclosures to the Financial Statements, RSI, and Stewardship Information.

The task force also considered the following areas of interest previously expressed by FASAB members:

- to explore ways of presenting information other than the standard financial statements, such as different levels of reporting for different users,

- to consider ways of providing simpler information on a more timely basis, such as quarterly, and

- to consider ways to communicate what is important on major spending programs.

The task force focused on the financial reporting model broadly rather than limiting its focus to only the aspects governed by FASAB accounting standards. Information that would be useful for the CFR should also inform consideration of the content of agency financial statements. Recognizing that the benefit to be obtained from federal financial reports is affected not only by the content of the reports but also by outreach to users and potential users, cultural factors, and delivery mechanisms (e.g., Internet transmission), the task force believed the broad view would be most helpful to FASAB, its sponsors, and the larger federal financial management community.

The task force formally met eight times and discussed these and other issues during the months of April, May, July, August, September, October, and November 2010. provides a list of the task force members, each of whom was selected based on their respective well-established backgrounds in federal financial reporting, primarily while in federal government service.[6] The task force membership included:

- the current Deputy CFO of the Department of the Treasury;

- the former Deputy CFO of the Department of Agriculture;

- the first Controller of the Office of Federal Financial Management in the Office of Management and Budget (OMB) and former FASAB member;

- a former senior leader from the Congressional Budget Office and also a former FASAB member;

- the former Assistant Comptroller General of the United States for Accounting and Information Management and Managing Director for Financial Management and Assurance at the Government Accountability Office (GAO);

---

[6] Additional background information is presented in Appendix II.

- the former staff director of the House Committee on Government Oversight;

- a former top OMB management official who was instrumental in establishing performance reporting concepts;

- the founder and CEO of the Institute for Truth in Accounting; and

- a partner in a major CPA firm, which audits a significant number of federal CFO Act agencies' financial statements, and who chairs the Certificate of Excellence in Accountability Reporting program sponsored by the Association of Government Accountants.

Introduction to Recommendations

The static, paper-based financial reports that the federal government delivers today contain important information about the financial health of the federal government. However, the reports are not presented and available in a way that engenders use, thereby limiting their impact. The federal government needs to make full use of modern technology to improve the presentation of information and adapt to the ways users want to receive information and are more likely to use the CFR.

This section provides further explanation of the task force recommendations to FASAB and its sponsors. It also includes illustrations of an enhanced reporting model and examples of a new Statement of Net Cost and the presentation of the Statement of Net Cost by function and department.

1. Adopt an Electronic, Web-Based Reporting Method

Move away from paper-based reporting and adopt an electronic, Web-based reporting method. The electronic, Web-based reporting method should be an integrated, highly interactive presentation that enables users to access financial information prepared in conformity with FASAB standards as well as under other reporting requirements of OMB, the Department of the Treasury, and federal law. An electronic, Web-based reporting method to provide a central source for federal financial information should be adopted and designed to permit users to "drill-down" to the appropriate level of detailed material.

In that regard, the Web site data should be machine-readable so that users can conduct searches and download the data in different formats. Also, a multimedia approach should be used to convey information so that citizens can understand its significance and how it affects them. A centralized site would help those users who are not familiar with the organizational structure of the U.S. government and the information made available to the public. By focusing on highly interactive financial information, the site would provide the variety of information that different users seek.

Changing the reporting method would resolve one concern with print-based financial reports; that is, the daunting number of pages required to provide comprehensive information about the federal government and its broad range of activities, and the challenge of navigating such printed reports to find specific information of interest to a particular user. For example, the note disclosures to the financial statements are an integral part of financial statements. However, they can be voluminous should an analyst or other user simply want to print a hard copy of the financial statements. To facilitate a streamlined presentation for users only seeking the financial statements, a Web site could have separate links for the financial statements and for the notes. Also, each page of the financial statements could have the statement, "the notes are an integral part of the financial statements," and a hyperlink[7] to the notes. In terms of navigating the current federal financial statements, there are no indexes or tools to search for information of specific interest. Task force members themselves, despite being extremely knowledgeable about the content of the CFR, sometimes find the report to be overly cumbersome and not easily navigated. For the broader target audience of citizens, the CFR is not something most can even begin to navigate in its present form, which was demonstrated in the results of the user needs survey.

Structuring the Web site with hyperlinks to additional information and "drill-down" capability could minimize the perceived burden associated with reading volumes of printed data. Some data is of limited interest to a particular user and may prevent the user from even finding what they were interested in or understanding the information if it is found. Essentially, a properly structured central Web site could provide users with access to information more efficiently than several print-based financial reports.

Recommended features of an electronic, Web-based reporting method also include:

- The use of a multimedia approach, such as a webcast to explain the nation's long-term fiscal challenges, which provides an opportunity not only to increase awareness but also understanding of complex information. The fiscal gap is so important to the public debate that the task force views this information as perhaps the most important being reported in the CFR and the companion Citizen's Guide.

- The ability to report government costs and accomplishments in a variety of ways based on user preferences

    - by function

    - by program

    - by region, state, or local jurisdiction

    - in time series

---

[7] The links could be designed to encourage additional research and educate users on federal government issues.

- The integration of financial and nonfinancial information important for demonstrating accountability and supporting decision-making is feasible through electronic reporting. The vastness of the federal government makes it very challenging to provide both a concise report and one that addresses accountability comprehensively. An electronic method can guide interested users to information while streamlining central reporting requirements.

- Electronic media could help reduce the potential for confusion caused by the current practice of presenting repetitive information in a printable document. For example, currently, the Citizen's Guide is published both as a stand-alone document and as a section of the Fiscal Year 2009 CFR. Because the Citizen's Guide repeats much of the information discussed in the MD&A section, readers of the CFR currently read the same information in two back-to-back sections. When using an electronic medium, the information in the Citizen's Guide could be presented on the central financial reporting Web site with hyperlinks to the CFR or could be a webcast with a reference to an integrated Web page that presents the detailed information currently provided in the printed CFR.

In addition, the Statement of the Acting Comptroller General of the United States (ACG Statement), on pages 31 to 38 of the Fiscal Year 2009 CFR, appears to discuss much of the same information presented in the Fiscal Year 2009 Citizen's Guide and MD&A. In addition, GAO provides a report, beginning on page 209 of the Fiscal Year 2009 CFR. Thus, readers may be confused by the presentation of what may be seen by some as two auditor reports.

When using electronic media, GAO could provide a multimedia presentation for citizens with a reference to an E-version[8] of the detailed auditor's report, and the E-auditor's report could have a hyperlink to the ACG's multimedia discussion. Also, after considering the full capabilities of electronic reporting, a determination could be made that only a single electronic presentation is necessary. Electronic media offers a variety of options to present views and facilitate users' understanding.

Moreover, an electronic method can provide the FASAB and its sponsors with timely metrics regarding users' interaction with the information. This would allow public officials to evaluate user needs based on their actions and better align the delivery of information with their needs. For example, FASAB will be able to determine how

---

[8] See the Government Accountability Office's pilot E-Report for an example.

many users visit a specific financial presentation, how much time they spend viewing it, and how many return visits are made.

Efforts to develop the electronic method should be undertaken now. Under the Open Government Directive, every federal department is currently seeking to make high-value data readily available to the public. With the user needs research that has already been conducted by FASAB and the high quality information readily available through annual audited financial reports, the FASAB and its sponsors should act quickly to utilize the technologies being developed under the directive. Waiting to introduce comprehensive financial reports to Open Government initiatives may limit opportunities for integration and use of existing resources available to support such initiatives.

For illustrative purposes, the task force developed a model that provides FASAB, budget, and performance information in multiple levels of aggregation, such as government-wide, department and agency, budget function, and activity. The illustrative model presents four layers of information–(1) an entry point, (2) key government-wide information, (3) a portal to agency sites, and (4) program-level information. Using layers and hyperlinks would help address the various types of information that different user groups seek, while integrating financial and nonfinancial information to facilitate context and understanding. Thus, citizens could go directly to the information they would commonly use or an analyst could digitally drill for information rather than searching various sources and manually compiling the data. A walk-through of the enhanced model is provided below.

<u>Layer 1: Entry Point</u>

A citizen would go to a central Web site for financial information about the federal government. The Web site would have tabs for various types of users such as citizens, analysts, Congress, or managers and executives. Each tab would direct the user to a Web page with information that they commonly seek. For example, a citizen would select the citizen's tab and could view an educational audio/visual presentation that describes the Web site and key terms and discusses information of general interest, such as the federal government's long-term fiscal outlook and the fiscal gap. Additionally, key terms could be explained as part of multimedia presentations throughout the model. Next, the citizen could click on a drop-down menu item for the federal government's long-term fiscal outlook and view a video on projected deficits and/or surpluses as a share of gross domestic product (GDP), or an interactive graph, and/or with audio explanations. By clicking a hyperlink on the graph, the citizen could view key information at the next layer.

<u>Layer 2: Key Government-wide Information</u>

This layer could provide key government-wide information. The citizen may view a Web page with information currently presented in the Citizen's Guide and a Web page with information presented in the CFR, such as an automated government-wide MD&A or other FASAB-based presentations. In addition, the Web pages could have links to information by budget function such as net costs, budgetary resources and outlays, and performance measures. Also, links to information about budget functions by agency and key programs within budget functions may be helpful.

"Plain language" could be used to describe these presentations and multimedia designed for online users would be featured.[9] For example, the citizen could listen to a podcast[10] discussion on new initiatives for functions. The citizen could also click on the information presented by function and identify the departments and agencies involved in managing the function.

<u>Layer 3: Portal to Department/Agency Sites</u>

The citizen could next enter the portal for departments and agencies. The citizen could view key information for the organization(s) of interest, such as the cost of selected programs and the results achieved. The agency's financial and performance information could be presented in this layer and enable an analyst to drill deeper than a citizen may desire. This layer could also feature information such as budget justifications, and policies or legislation under consideration.

<u>Layer 4: Program-Level Information</u>

Layer 4 could provide program-level information. For example, the layer could provide data related to Recovery Act spending, federal spending on grants and contracts, or data on the geographic distribution of federal program expenditures.

Web-based surveys could be built into the model to identify the most commonly sought information and the structure of the model could be revised to better accommodate users' interests.
provides an illustration of the enhanced model for discussion purposes.

---

[9] Online users may not wish to read a significant amount of text, as is currently included in printed documents. To help improve readability, the use of headings, colors, and graphics would need to increase.
[10] The links could be designed to encourage additional research and educate users on federal government issues.

2. Explore How Best to Report Additional Government-wide Performance Information

Explore how best to report additional government-wide performance information in the MD&A of the CFR or in another electronic government-wide presentation. Statement of Federal Financial Accounting Standards 15, *Management's Discussion and Analysis*, provides guidance for reporting information in the MD&A. Among other items, it states that the MD&A should address the entity's program and financial performance and deal with the most important matters that will likely affect users' judgments and decisions, such as decisions about the efficiency and effectiveness of the federal government. Also, the CFO Act's requirements point toward improved financial information available to agency management, Congress, and others. The CFO Act calls for the systematic measurement of performance, the development of cost information, and the integration of systems–program, budget, and accounting. In addition to improved accountability and transparency, expanded reporting of program performance information can provide indicators of potential problems before they develop into more challenging issues and can be a tool to help manage the cost of government as envisioned by the framers of the CFO Act.[11]

Currently, the nation is engaged in discussions involving the efficiency and effectiveness of government and information prepared in conformity with established standards should be most useful to inform those debates. Reporting government-wide program performance in the CFR would help users assess: the impact of alternative courses of action, the economy and efficiency of government operations, and the government's effectiveness in attaining planned goals.

3. Present a Functional Statement of Net Cost in the CFR with Departmental Net Cost by Function as RSI

Present net cost by function and in comparison to spending (outlays) and present net cost by budget function and department (or agency) in RSI. The Statement of Net Cost (SNC) shows the cost to operate the federal government, and currently presents the costs by agency and in total. FASAB focus group discussions with citizens indicated that users are more likely to focus on the government's functions rather than the agencies responsible for administering them. Functions present information in terms of the principal national need the programs are intended to serve, and each program is related to a single functional category that best

---

[11] Association of Government Accountants, "The CFO Act Turns 20 Years Old: As We Blow Out the Candles, Where Are We Today and Where Do We Go From Here" and "CFO Act 20 Years Later – Perspectives of the First Controller," *Journal of Government Financial Management*, Winter 2010 Vol.59, No. 4

represents its major purpose, regardless of the entity that administers it.[12] In addition, Congress and federal government leaders are familiar with the function classifications.

The relationship between net costs and budgetary amounts or outlays[13] should also be presented. Outlay data, now reported through Web sites such as Recovery.gov and USAspending.gov, provide only the budgetary perspective. Helping users understand and compare the amount spent on and the net cost of each function would provide citizens with information for assessing the federal government's financial performance in relation to its budget and help clarify the difference between budget and net cost in financial statements.

A concise explanation of the differences between these two bases of accounting should facilitate their comparison and increase awareness of future cash flow requirements that will arise as a result of current operations. Such comparisons are part of the state and local government financial reporting model and the reporting models employed by other countries, such as Canada, New Zealand, and the United Kingdom. To accommodate this additional detail, the SNC would no longer present gross cost and earned revenue. Instead, only net cost would be required. See for an illustration.

Moreover, the task force recognizes that the departmental information provided in the current SNC provides an important link to departmental reports for users desiring more information. This presentation would allow users to identify the departments most relevant to the functions of interest to them. Accordingly, net cost by budget function and department or agency should be presented in RSI. See

for an illustration.

4. Establish Minimum Requirements for a Statement of Spending

Establish the minimum requirements for a Statement of Spending. The task force understands that the CFO Council is developing a Statement of Spending for agencies. We support this initiative and recommend that, at a minimum, a Statement of Spending for agencies and for inclusion in the government-wide CFR present: (a) where and how tax dollars are being spent, (b) how spending data

---

[12] GAO, *A Glossary of Terms Used in the Federal Budget Process* (Washington, D.C.: 2005).

[13] An outlay is a payment to liquidate an obligation (other than the repayment of debt principal). Outlays generally are equal to cash disbursements but also are recorded for cash-equivalent transactions, such as federal employee salaries and debt instruments. In addition, outlays are the measure of government spending.

relates to net cost data, and (c) an explanation of the differences between these two bases of reporting.

5. Include Intergovernmental Financial Dependency in RSI

Include summary-level information on intergovernmental financial dependency in RSI. Intergovernmental financial dependency is the reliance of one level of government on another level for direct financial flows, or indirect financial flows derived from the purchases of goods and services and/or payments to individuals within a governmental jurisdiction by another level of government. Such dependency can also be associated with the holding of the financial obligations of one level of government by another as an income-producing asset. As elaborated below, such intergovernmental financial dependency, organized by state, should be reported as RSI.

The federal government is dependent on state and local government to carry out and administer a wide range of federal programs, costing over $500 billion annually, not counting Recovery Act funding. Also, the federal government is typically the largest employer and purchaser of goods and services in many states. The federal government's impact on a state's gross domestic product is significant–on the order of 30 percent for one state where the impact was studied.[14]

States and local governments face their own long-term fiscal challenges, and these challenges add to the nation's overall fiscal struggles.[15] To the extent state and local governments face fiscal challenges that impair their ability to carry out federal programs or otherwise meet obligations to their citizens, there is a fiscal risk to the federal government as demonstrated by the hundreds of billions of dollars of recovery funding provided to state and local governments. And conversely, to the extent the federal government reduces its spending in response to its own fiscal gap, state and local governments' financial condition will be significantly impacted.

Federal financial reporting objectives require information on the financial condition of the federal government and that of the nation to help users assess the impact of the federal government on the country.[16] To help achieve these reporting objectives, RSI should include a schedule that summarizes the extent of intergovernmental financial dependency by disclosing (1) total direct grants and flows to state

---

[14] Edward J. Mazur, *Intergovernmental Financial Dependency and Related Risks.* (Richmond, Virginia, Cherry, Bekaert & Holland, LLP., 2009).
[15] See GAO-10-358.
[16] See

governments; (2) total direct grants and flows to local governments summarized by state; (3) total federal purchases from businesses summarized by state; and (4) total direct payments to individuals within the jurisdiction of each state for Social Security, Medicare, federal retirement, and disability payments—both civilian and military, and federal salaries and wages—both civilian and military. Also, the total of such direct and indirect flows as a percentage of combined state GDP should be provided as well as a summary of Federal Treasury Securities held at year end by state and local governments and their respective pension funds. The electronic reporting method should provide hyperlinks to this information.

6. Enhance the Information Value of the Reconciliation of Net Operating Cost and Unified Budget Deficit Statement through Re-labeling

Re-label the Reconciliation of Net Operating Cost and Unified Budget Deficit Statement so that the statement will be more understandable to users. The statement presents how net operating cost prepared on an accrual basis relates to the unified budget deficit. Accrual and budgetary accounting share significant amounts of data and the reconciliation shows the differences between the two. The statement shows the amount of net operating costs attributable to civilian and military employee benefits, depreciation of assets, and how much the federal government invested in capital assets during the period.

However, the general public may consider that the term "budget" indicates a plan, and it is not clear whether the accrual net cost amounts are being reconciled to planned expenditures or actual outlays. Also, it is not readily apparent whether line items should be added or subtracted from Net Operating Cost to derive the Unified Budget Deficit. Inserting headings such as "add excess of expenses over budget outlays" may help readers understand which amounts are included or not included in the Unified Budget Deficit. The form of the statement presented as illustrated in SFFAS 24, *Selected Standards for the Consolidated Financial Report of the United States Government*, Appendix B: Illustrative Statement: Reconciliation, is a good example of a Reconciliation of Net Operating Cost and Unified Budget Deficit Statement.

7. Reclassify the Information in the Statement of Changes in Cash Balance from Unified Budget and Other Activities

Reclassify the Statement of Changes in Cash Balance from Unified Budget and Other Activities from a basic financial statement to a schedule in the notes or RSI. The statement provides an operational context for the financial statements and its information may be important for only a limited number of users. It presents the relationship among the unified budget deficit and the change in the federal government's cash balance and debt held by the public. The statement is intended to help readers understand why the unified budget deficit would not necessarily result in a change in the federal government's cash balance.[17] This is most likely of interest to specialists rather than generalists. Because FASAB's concepts for financial reporting provide for the Board to consider whether information under consideration for inclusion in basic information is of interest to a wide audience or specialists, the task force suggests moving this information.[18]

To help streamline the basic statements presented in the CFR, the information in the Statement of Changes in Cash Balance from Unified Budget and Other Activities could be considered for presentation as a schedule in the notes or in RSI, depending upon consideration of its importance relative to understanding the government's financial position.

8. Re-orient the Balance Sheet Display and Enhance Related MD&A Discussion

Re-orient the format of the balance sheet such that the "bottom line" is "net position." This re-oriented Balance Sheet would illustrate the federal government's assets and liabilities and net position, that is, the arithmetic difference between assets and liabilities. The current CFR balance sheet format, presented in the MD&A and in the financial statement section, totals assets, then liabilities and net position are totaled and the two totals are equal. Thus, it focuses on the following accounting equation:

$$Assets = liabilities + net\ position$$

As an alternative, the information should be presented consistent with the following equation:

$$Assets - liabilities = net\ position$$

This format leaves net position as the last number on the statement. This format helps focus the reader's attention on the comparison of assets and liabilities and the resulting net position. This focus may be most helpful for analyzing the present financial position under FASAB standards relative to fiscal gap.

---

[17] Statement of Federal Financial Accounting Standards (SFFAS) 24, *Selected Standards for the Consolidated Financial Report of the United States Government*, par. 31.
[18] Statement of Federal Financial Accounting Concepts (SFFAC) 2, *Entity and Display* (as amended), par. 73E.c.

In addition, the discussion on assets (page 42 of the Fiscal Year 2009 CFR) could be enhanced to inform readers what the assets signify to the operations of the government. Also, the discussion on Liabilities and Net Position (page 42 of the Fiscal Year 2009 CFR) could discuss who the stakeholders are in relation to specific liabilities, as well as their reliance on the government's reliable recognition of those liabilities.

9. Explain the Difference Between Net Position and Fiscal Gap

Add explanatory text to the balance sheet to help readers understand the difference between net position and fiscal gap. FASAB's financial reporting objectives require information on both the government's financial position and whether future budgetary resources will likely be sufficient to sustain services and meet obligations as they come due. To help achieve these objectives, the CFR includes a balance sheet to provide a "point-in-time" view of the federal government's financial health and, beginning in Fiscal Year 2010, the CFR also presents fiscal gap information. Fiscal gap information presents long-term projections of cash flows to provide a "forward-looking" view. Forward-looking information is most helpful to policymakers as an early warning given the considerable time required to enact policy changes and to provide a window into the long-term fiscal impacts of delaying policy changes.

Both perspectives, point-in-time and forward-looking information, are essential to CFR users in assessing where the federal government's financial health stands currently and where it is likely headed in the long-term absent a policy change. Adding a note to the balance sheet explaining net position and fiscal gap would assist users in understanding the need for both amounts in the CFR. The task force applauds the actions of FASAB to include fiscal gap information and the Statement of Social Insurance in the CFR. We view this type of information as having the utmost of importance to users in understanding the true financial condition of the federal government. The balance sheet must be looked at in context of the additional long-term commitments captured in the fiscal gap and on the Statement of Social Insurance.

10. Establish a Federal Financial Information Web Site and Raise Awareness of Federal Financial Information

Establish a central Web site for federal financial information and inform the public of its availability. Ultimately, the success of the previous recommendations requires adequately raising public awareness of federal financial reports and the information they provide. Currently, the public is not aware that financial reports exist and some groups are building their own federal financial information Web sites to inform public

debates. For example, the site http://www.annualreportusa.com/ displays an
"Annual Report of the United States of America," and is prepared by the Harvard
Political Review. The site is intended to provide the "average citizen" with a view of
how and why the federal government spends tax dollars. However, the site does not
refer to the CFR or the basis for presenting the information. Another site,
http://www.usgovernmentspending.com/ provides federal, state, and local spending
information, but does not discuss the differences between cost and spending and
accomplishments.   Accordingly, diverse Web sites and information sources that
portray the distribution of "federal" financial information can be confusing to the
public at a vital time in planning our nation's fiscal future. It is important that the
federal government have a way to make its financial and program results readily
available. This recommendation ties directly to recommendation 1, Adopt an
Electronic Web-Based Reporting Method.

As an initial approach to addressing the above issues, a prototype Web site should
be developed. A prototype would enable the federal government to take advantage
of existing technologies and help identify improvements that may be needed when
the Web site becomes fully functional. For example, the prototype would be used to
test the design of the site for ease of access and the types of visual presentations
that may be most effective. Also, metrics should be collected to learn more about
users and the information that they are seeking.

In addition, a government-wide initiative would be needed to make the public aware
of the Web site. While educating the public on the federal sources for financial
information about their government, the awareness initiative would: help the public
know about the existence of federal financial information prepared in conformity with
FASAB standards; help disseminate information on the federal government's
financial condition and the accomplishments of programs; encourage a broader base
of users of federal financial information; and help potential users understand and use
the various features of the Web site.

The task force would like to recognize the outstanding support it received from Ross Simms, FASAB Assistant Director. Ross' professionalism, steady hand, and vast knowledge of federal financial reporting were important assets to the task force. It was a privilege to work with Ross. We would also like to thank Wendy Payne for her outstanding participation in a number of our task force meetings and steadfast support to advancing federal financial reporting.

Since its inception in 1990, FASAB has continued to make important contributions to improving federal government accountability and transparency. The members of the task force appreciated the opportunity to contribute to FASAB's important work and to provide this report and recommendations.

Federal financial reporting objectives consider the information needs of users and guide the FASAB in developing accounting standards. Also, the objectives provide a framework for assessing existing financial reporting systems and considering how new standards might enhance accountability and decisionmaking. The four financial reporting objectives are presented in Table 1: Objectives of Federal Financial Reporting.

Table 1: Objectives of Federal Financial Reporting

Budgetary Integrity—Federal financial reporting should assist in fulfilling the government's duty to be publicly accountable for monies raised through taxes and other means and for their expenditure in accordance with the appropriations laws that establish the government's budget for a particular fiscal year and related laws and regulations. Federal financial reporting should provide information that helps the reader to determine:

•how budgetary resources have been obtained and used and whether their acquisition and use were in accordance with the legal authorization,

•the status of budgetary resources, and

•how information on the use of budgetary resources relates to information on the costs of program operations and whether information on the status of budgetary resources is consistent with other accounting information on assets and liabilities.

Operating Performance—Federal financial reporting should assist report users in evaluating the service efforts, costs, and accomplishments of the reporting entity; the manner in which these efforts and accomplishments have been financed; and the management of the entity's assets and liabilities. Federal financial reporting should provide information that helps the reader to determine:

•the costs of providing specific programs and activities and the composition of, and changes in, these costs;

•the efforts and accomplishments associated with federal programs and the changes over time and in relation to costs; and

•the efficiency and effectiveness of the government's management of its assets and liabilities.

Stewardship—Federal financial reporting should assist report users in assessing the impact on the country of the government's operations and investments for the period and how, as a result, the government's and the nation's financial condition has changed and may change in the future. Federal financial reporting should provide information that helps the reader to determine whether

•the government's financial position improved or deteriorated over the period,

•future budgetary resources will likely be sufficient to sustain public services and to meet obligations as they come due, and

•government operations have contributed to the nation's current and future well-being.

Systems and Control—Federal financial reporting should assist report users in understanding whether financial management systems and internal accounting and administrative controls are adequate to ensure that

•transactions are executed in accordance with budgetary and financial laws and other requirements, consistent with the purposes authorized, and are recorded in accordance with federal accounting standards;

•assets are properly safeguarded to deter fraud, waste, and abuse; and

•performance measurement information is adequately supported.

Source: SFFAC 1, Objectives of Federal Financial Reporting.

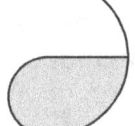

- Jonathan D. Breul, Executive Director, IBM Center for The Business of Government, and Partner, IBM's Global Business Services

- Patricia E. Healy, Executive Consultant, CGI

- Michael J. Hettinger, Executive Director of Practice Planning and Marketing, Global Public Sector, Grant Thornton LLP

- John H. Hummel, Partner and Federal Segment Leader, KPMG LLP

- Edward J. Mazur, Senior Advisor for Public Sector Services, Clifton Gunderson LLP

- Marvin Phaup, Director, Federal Budget Reform Initiative, Pew Charitable Trusts

- Al Runnels, Deputy Chief Financial Officer, Department of the Treasury

- Jeffrey C. Steinhoff, Executive Director, KPMG Government Institute, and Managing Director, KPMG LLP

- Sheila A. Weinberg, founder and CEO, the Institute for Truth in Accounting

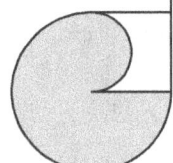

Citizens' Views about Content

In addition to views about how financial information should be provided, citizens discussed what information they believed is important. They generally believed that information currently found in financial reports is important. For example, existing performance and accountability reports present information on results, liabilities, cost, and assets. Also, the financial statements are independently audited. Figure 1: Additional National Survey Results shows the results of our national survey on the information that citizens believed is important to know about the federal government. This information helped inform the work and considerations of the Task Force.

Figure 1: Additional National Survey Results

Additional National Survey Results

77% believed that understandable results information is very/extremely important

67% believed that understandable liabilities information is very/extremely important

64% believed that understandable cost information is very/extremely important

63% believed that providing independently audited or verified financial information is very/extremely important

61% believed that understandable financial information about individual agencies and departments is very/extremely important

58% believed that understandable asset information is very/extremely important

FASAB Members' Perspectives

In establishing the Task Force, the members of the FASAB authored a series of questions, suggested lines of inquiry, and offered ideas pertaining to the federal reporting model. This thinking was documented by FASAB staff and helped inform the work and considerations of the Task Force.

Task Force Approach

At its first meeting, the task force identified the following concerns and ideas:

Financial Report Presentation and Reconsideration of Financial Statements

Federal financial information should be presented electronically and be understandable. Additionally, the task force should not necessarily seek to add more data to that already being provided or be confined to traditional financial statements. Financial statements are essential for any democratic society, but they may not produce, alone, the mechanism necessary to cause decision makers to act. Providing information in electronic form would permit users to select items of information from a menu, perform drill-downs to more detailed information, and extract and array the data into the information they desire. A lot of these data may have been audited as part of a financial or performance audit. Utilizing electronic technology allows individuals to decide on the information they need, such as the cost of programs. Also, visualizations and graphic tools should be used to communicate the information which would be consistent with current trends where individuals are reading "tweets" that are 140 characters or less in length and viewing videos to satisfy their information needs.

Intended Audience for the Government-wide Report and Need for Educating Potential Users

The focus of the project should be on providing information to the public, primarily those willing to educate themselves on federal financial matters. This would contribute to Congress' needs because they are concerned about the information that their constituents want. This group would include governors and elected local officials, investors in Treasury securities, those who are planning their financial future, think thanks, and concerned citizens groups. Also, there is a need to consider that citizens seem to care about broad numbers, like pension liabilities, and how those numbers impact them. The Governmental Accounting Standards Board (GASB) Statement 34, *Basic Financial Statements and Management's*

Discussion and Analysis for State and Local Governments, paragraph 185, provides core values that could be considered as part of the project.

Information That Should Be Presented

The key information that should be provided includes forward-looking information, explanations to help users understand the context of the reported information, explanations of the relationship of the federal government's operations to other levels of government, businesses, and the public, discussions on the positive and negative impact on the public of government programs and the fiscal gap, and a presentation of the top programs or delivery mechanisms. The federal government should be able to tell its "story" to the public and useful financial information provides individuals with information on what current policies imply about the future. The public wants to know how much the federal government received, how much was spent, and what the federal government obtained for what was spent.

Other Items

Other matters noted included the following:

The data being sought should have integrity and be neutral, i.e., no conclusions as to policy or program drawn.

A goal should be to reduce the cost of citizens' access to information and increase its value to them.

The task force noted that the MD&A standards discuss forward-looking information and the FASAB's work on fiscal sustainability and social insurance included a component to change the MD&A at CFR level. The standards for the CFR MD&A require key numbers from basic financial statements to be presented in a central location and have narrative explanation. However, the consensus of the FASAB has been not to be too prescriptive in the standards. This would allow a level of flexibility as circumstances change.

Given the need to take action promptly, the task force decided to focus on the summary-level information of the CFR, i.e., the Citizen's Guide and MD&A sections and organize a subgroup to consider the government-wide financial statements. FASAB staff could begin to identify what information should be presented and improvements needed for presenting the information at the summary levels by looking at how the media present government financial information.

FASAB staff completed an analysis of news sources citing the CFR using its official title, *Financial Report of the United States Government*. The purpose of the analysis was to determine the news sources that are likely to cite the document and inform the public about its contents. Using Nexis to search for news sources that referred to the report during the 5-year period ending June 2, 2010, the task force noted that press releases, blogs, and congressional testimony are the news sources likely to inform the public about information presented in the report.

In addition, FASAB staff completed interviews with 15 state and local government officials located in 14 states. The purpose of the interviews was to determine what federal financial information state and local government planners need and how the summary sections of the CFR can be improved. State and local government respondents primarily sought information on the amount of money the federal government provides to states, local governments, and to others. They would like to know what areas of the country receive federal dollars and why. This information would assist them in planning their programs, developing their budgets, and comparing their performance with others. Also, staff noted that only six of the respondents had reviewed the CFR. As a result, no themes on what information they found useful or interesting in the report could be developed.

Layer 1 – Entry Point

Layer 1 is the entry point. Users enter the Web site which presents current efforts and accomplishments, long-term opportunities and challenges, key national indicators, and broad risks (intergovernmental dependency). This layer includes costs and accomplishments by function, uses graphics and illustrations, and dollar amounts are expressed as a percentage of GDP. Figure 2: Layer 1 illustration provides an example of the type of information that may be included at the entry point. Users can scroll through different graphics and click on the listed topics for additional information. Also, this page could have tabs for specific users, i.e., citizens, Congress, and analysts, and direct them to other levels or information that they typically seek. Citizens may seek information on programs of the greatest interest such as Social Security, Medicare/Medicaid, and national defense, while analysts may be interested in budgetary trends and projections.

Figure 2: Layer 1 illustration

FASAB Accountability is the U.S. government's official website that provides easy access to information related to current and long-term financial conditions.

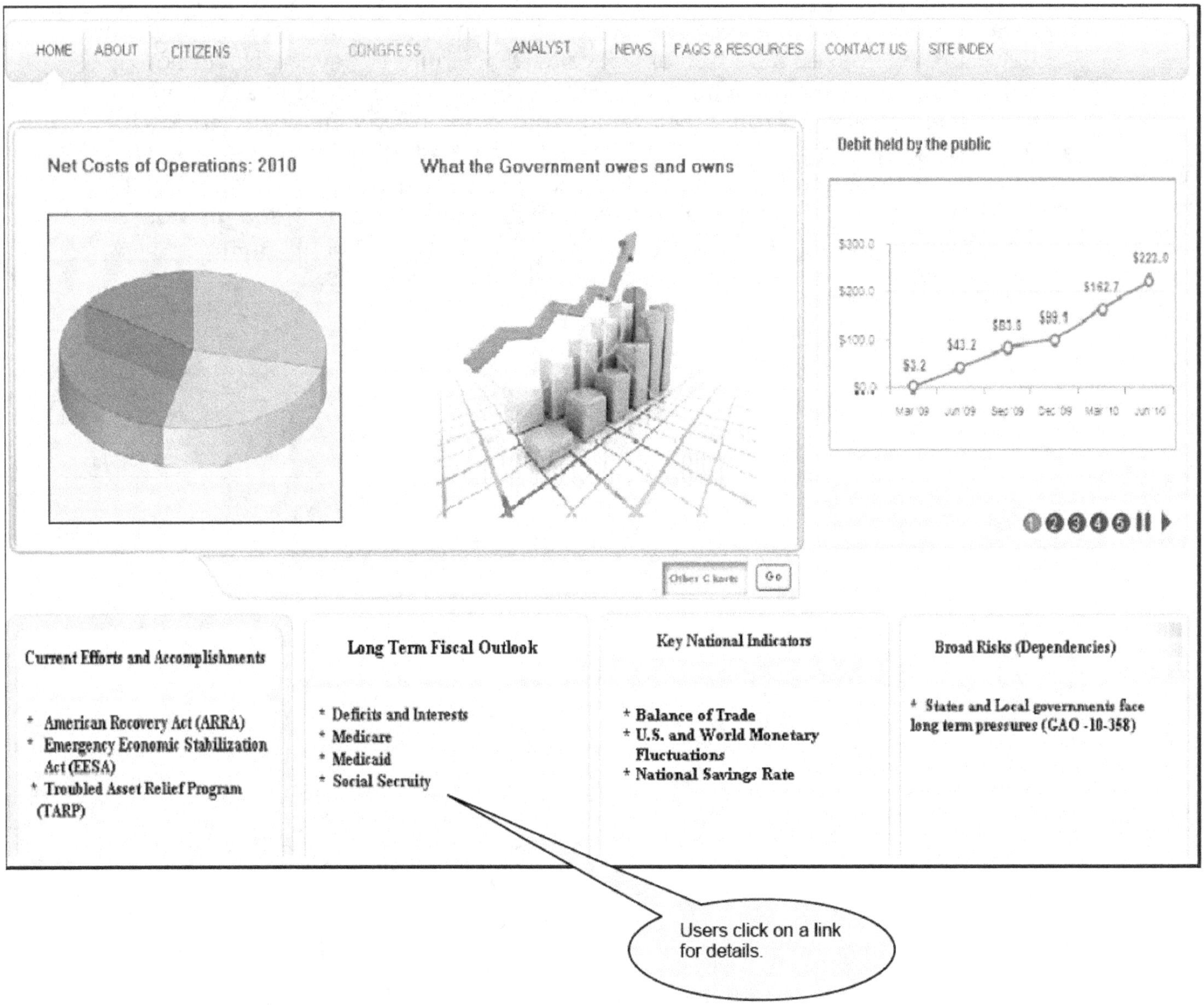

HOME   ABOUT   CITIZENS   CONGRESS   ANALYST   NEWS   FAQS & RESOURCES   CONTACT US   SITE INDEX

Net Costs of Operations: 2010   What the Government owes and owns   Debit held by the public

$300.0
$200.0 $222.0
$100.0 $162.7
$0.0 $3.2 $43.2 $83.6 $99.1
Mar 09   Jun 09   Sep 09   Dec 09   Mar 10   Jun 10

①②③④⑤ II ▶

Other Charts   [Go]

Current Efforts and Accomplishments

* American Recovery Act (ARRA)
* Emergency Economic Stabilization Act (EESA)
* Troubled Asset Relief Program (TARP)

Long Term Fiscal Outlook

* Deficits and Interests
* Medicare
* Medicaid
* Social Security

Key National Indicators

* Balance of Trade
* U.S. and World Monetary Fluctuations
* National Savings Rate

Broad Risks (Dependencies)

* States and Local governments face long term pressures (GAO -10-358)

Users click on a link for details.

Layer 2 – Key Government-wide Information

Layer 2 provides key government-wide information. Users can view a Web page with information currently presented in the Citizen's Guide and a Web page with information presented in the CFR, such as an automated government-wide MD&A or other FASAB-based presentations. In addition the Web pages could have links to information by budget function about net costs, budgetary resources and outlays, and performance measures, and links to information about budget functions by agency and key programs within budget functions. The integrated financial presentation would include links among its components and to data outside of the presentation. Given the broad array of information needed to help users understand the federal government's activities, integrated links would assist them in navigating and locating the information they need. The information would also be presented on the Web in layers. This would facilitate a streamlined presentation because users would simply view the data they choose. Figure 3: Layer 2 illustration provides an example of the types of information to be included in Layer 2.

Figure 3: Layer 2 illustration

Layer 3 – Portal to Agency Sites

Layer 3 provides a portal to the many federal departments and agencies and the immense information and data they present. The Agency Portal Access (illustrated on page 37), guides the user to a list of agencies as, illustrated in Figure 4: Layer 3 Example. Upon selecting the agency and viewing key information, the user would be able to access additional information and data in Layer 4.

AGENCY PORTAL ACCESS

Figure 4: Layer 3 Example

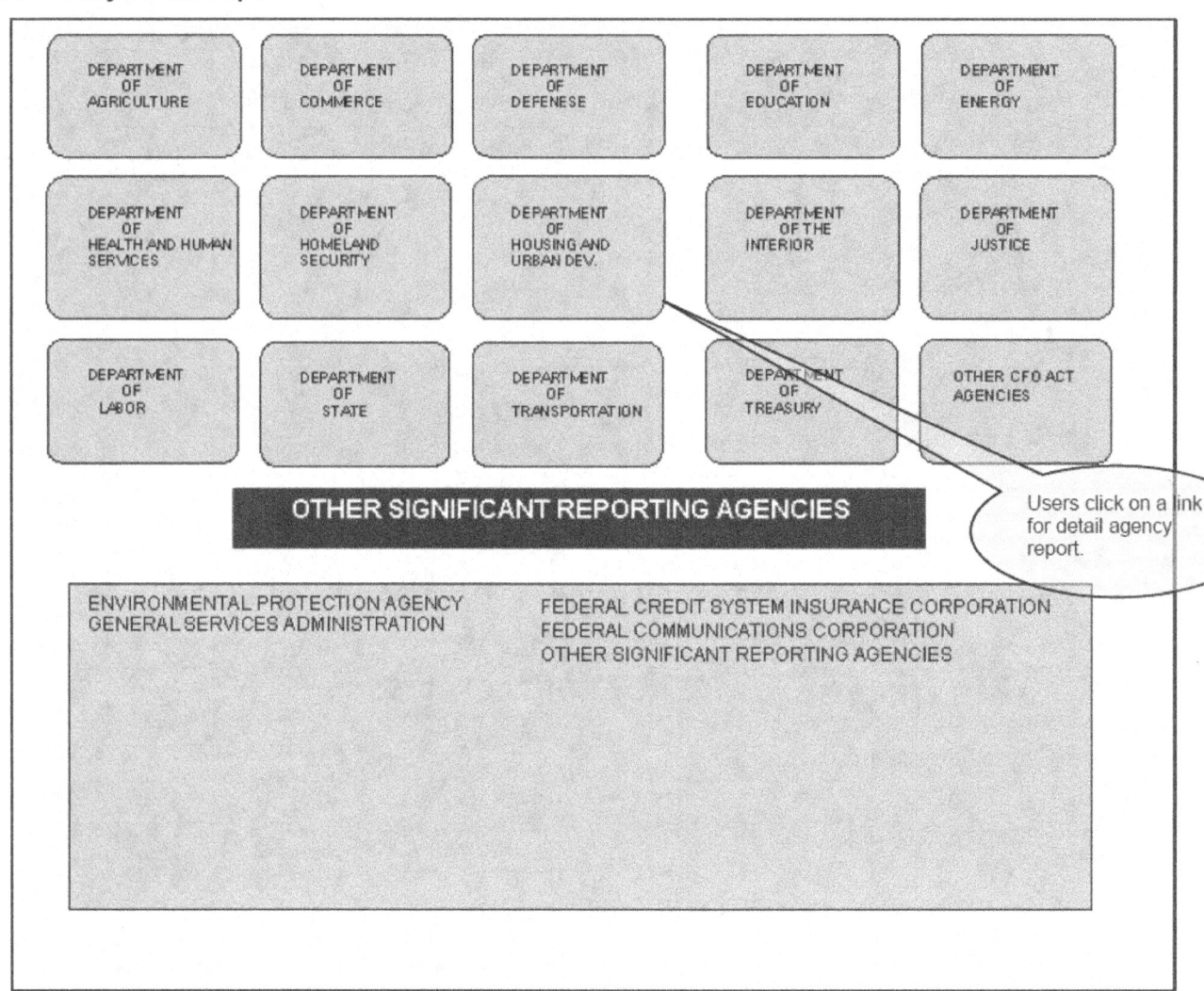

The agency pages would include performance and financial information. Also, a key agency information Web page can be added.

Layer 3 – Agency Reports Continued

Figure 5: Agency Reports Illustration

Source: Hud.gov

Users click on a link for detail agency report.

Figure 6: Agency Report Illustration Continued

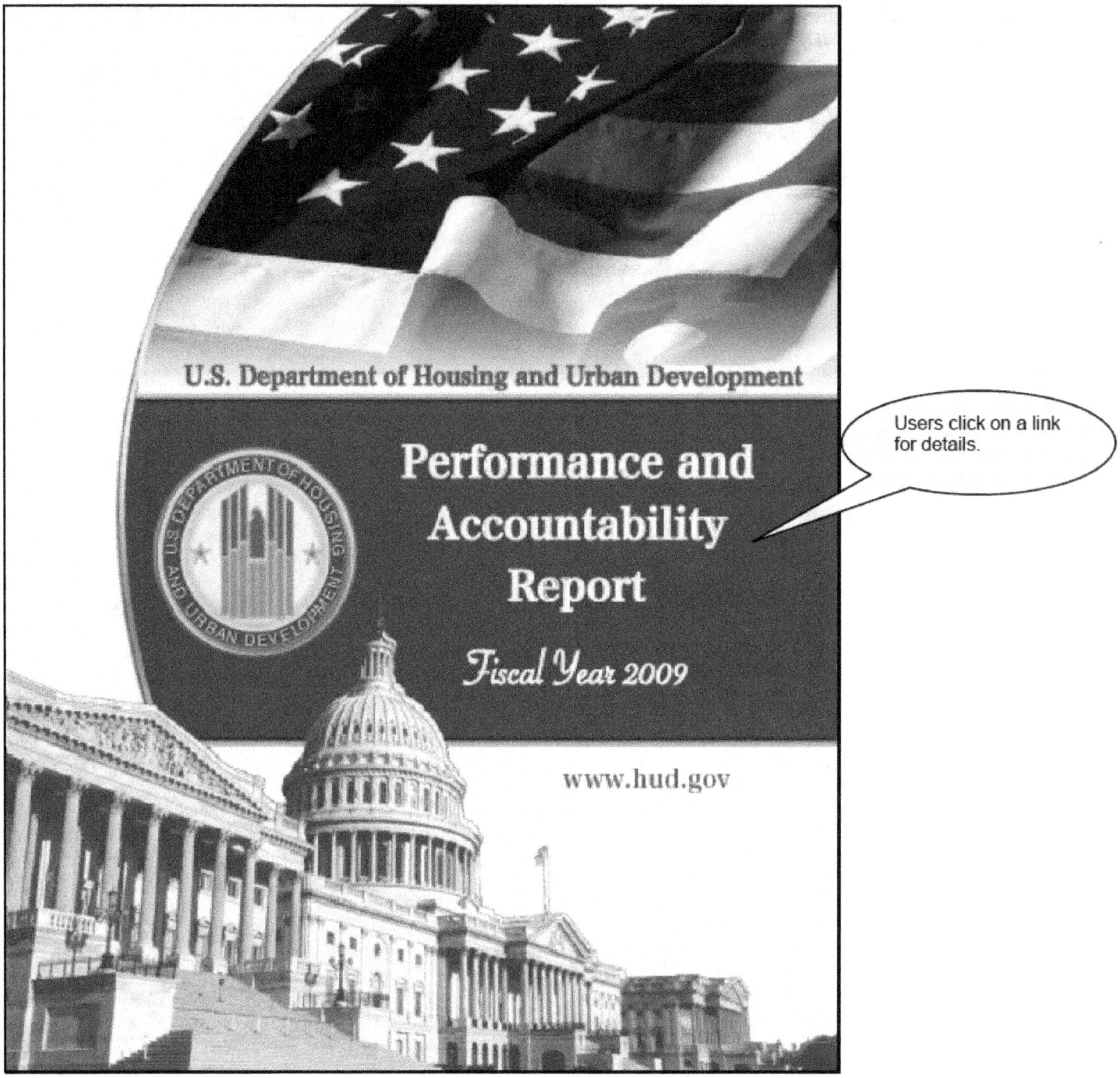

Source: Hud.gov

Layer 4 – Program-Level Information

Layer 4 could provide data related to Recovery Act spending, federal spending on grants and contracts, data on the geographic distribution of federal program expenditures, and/or other information deemed on interest. See the following examples.

Figure 7: Illustration of Recovery Data

Source: Recovery.gov

Figure 8: Illustration of Spending Data

Source: USAspending.gov

Figure 9: Illustration of Consolidated Federal Funds Report

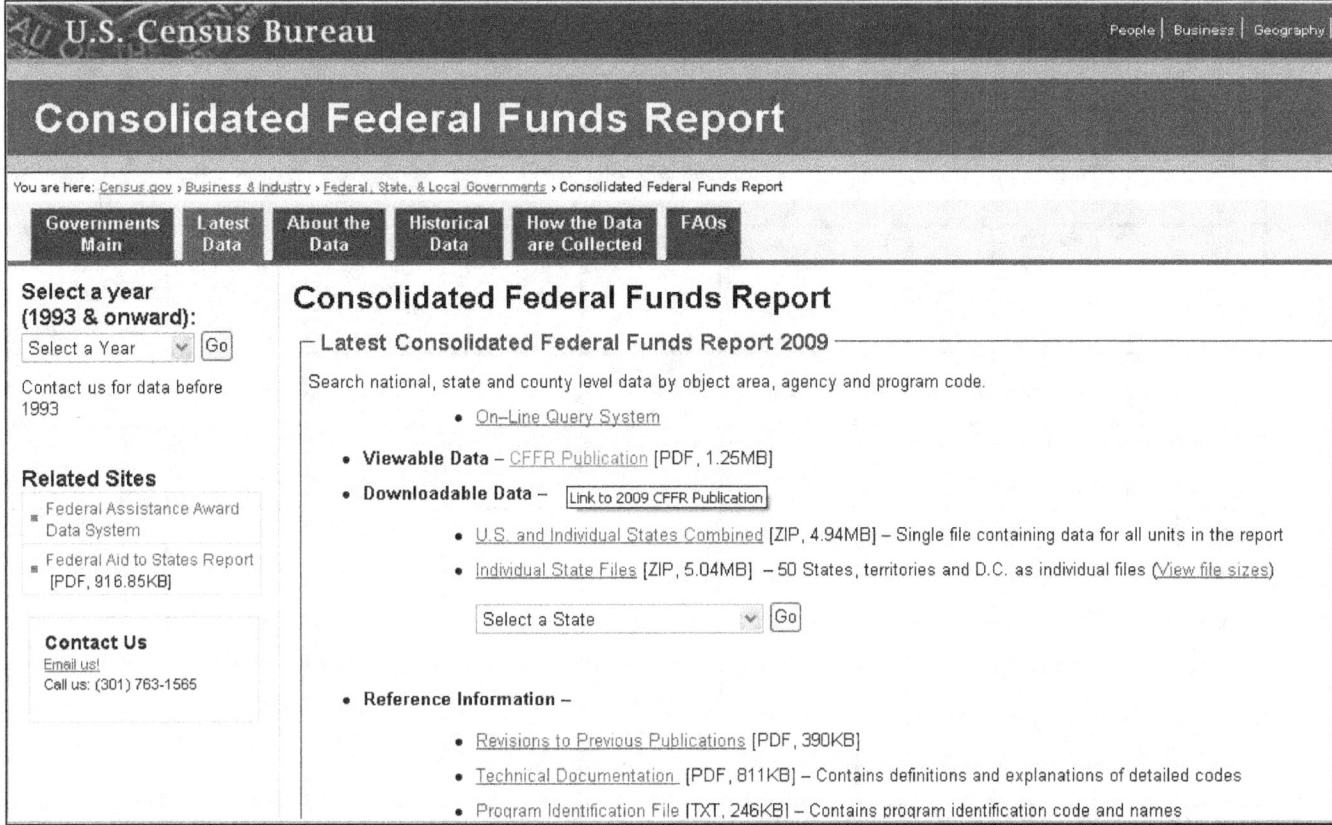

Source: Census.gov

Budget function	2009				2008			
	Budget outlays	Plus net cost included in past budgets	Plus net cost to be included in future budgets	Resulting net cost	Budget outlays	Plus net cost included in past budgets	Plus net cost to be included in future budgets	Resulting net cost
National defense								
Human resources								
Education, training, employment, and social services								
Health								
Medicare								
Income security								
Social Security								
Other budget functions								
Total								

Appendix VI: Example Presentation of Statement of Net Cost by Function and Department

Net Cost by Budget Function and Department/Agency

Department/agency	National defense	Human Resources					Other budget functions	Net interest	Total
		Education, training, employment, and social services	Health	Medicare	Income security	Social Security			
Department of Health and Human Services									
Social Security Administration									
Department of Defense									
Department of the Treasury									
Other Departments/Agencies									
Total									

www.ingramcontent.com/pod-product-compliance
Lightning Source LLC
Chambersburg PA
CBHW080625290526
45790CB00007B/2929